The
Holy Family

W9-BEN-388

REV. JUDE WINKLER, OFM Conv.

Imprimi Potest: Michael Kolodziej, OFM Conv., Minister Provincial of St. Anthony of Padua Province (USA)
Nihil Obstat: Sr. M. Kathleen Flanagan, S.C., Ph.D., Censor Librorum
Imprimatur: ✠ **Frank J. Rodimer, J.C.D.**, Bishop of Paterson

The Nihil Obstat and Imprimatur are official declarations that a book or pamphlet is free of doctrinal or moral error. No impli-
cation is contained therein that those who have granted the Nihil Obstat and Imprimatur agree with the contents, opinions or
statements expressed.

© 2003 by CATHOLIC BOOK PUBLISHING CORP., Totowa, N.J.
Printed in Hong Kong

ISBN 978-0-89942-527-6

Mary and Joseph Engaged

THERE is a saying that if you want to get to know someone, then you should get to know that person's family. That is why we want to know more about the Holy Family of Jesus, so that we will know more about Him.

The parents of Mary were Joachim and Anne. We are not sure who Joseph's parents were. The Gospel of Matthew tells us that his father's name was Jacob, while the Gospel of Luke tells us that it was Eli. Maybe his father had two names, like Simon Peter. We know even less about Joseph's mother because we do not even know her name.

Joseph and Mary were probably from the same town, and their families would have arranged for them to meet. They would then have discussed how much Joseph owned and what Mary was expected to bring into the marriage. Then, there would be a special ceremony to make the engagement official. This usually happened about a year before they were to be wed.

Once the couple was engaged, they were as good as being married. It was a very special promise. They were not yet man and wife, but they were expected to get ready for their wedding. They were to be faithful to each other and learn to love one another.

The Annunciation

THERE was so much to prepare before the couple could get married. They would have to think of their clothing and dishes and a million other things. But the most important chore was to make sure that there was enough food to host the entire village. They were expected to invite everyone to the wedding feast.

While Mary and Joseph were still engaged, the Archangel Gabriel appeared to Mary. He greeted her by saying that she was "full of grace." This greeting was a way of saying that Mary was truly the Immaculate Conception. She had been preserved from sin and all the damage that it causes from the moment that she was conceived. She, of all the people who ever lived, was truly holy. This is why God had sent Gabriel to Mary to ask her to be the mother of His Son.

But Mary was confused by the angel's greeting and even more by this request. She had never slept with a man; she was a virgin. How could she become a mother?

The angel assured her that nothing is impossible with God. Mary's cousin, Elizabeth, whom everyone thought could never have a baby, was now pregnant—in her sixth month. If God could do this miracle, then God could surely give Mary a Child.

Joseph's Dream

THIS was all very confusing for Mary, but it seems to have been even more confusing for Joseph. He was engaged to Mary. She was to be his wife and his alone. Now he found out that she was pregnant. He had trusted her, and he must have felt that she had betrayed that trust.

The law of Israel was very clear in this situation. She was to be put to death. But Joseph was a good and gentle and compassionate man. He could not stand the thought of Mary receiving that punishment.

Joseph decided that it would be better if he divorced Mary. Remember, even though they were only engaged to each other, it was as if they were already married. But this would still be very difficult for Mary. She could never be married to anyone else because she would have had a Child outside of marriage. People would gossip about her and probably call her bad names. Still, at least, she would be alive.

But God taught Joseph to be more merciful than he thought he could be. God sent an angel to Joseph in a dream to tell him not to worry. The Child that Mary was going to have was conceived by the Holy Spirit. Joseph was to take Mary home and care for her as he would care for a wife. He would be the foster father of the Child to be born.

Jesus Is Born

MARY, instead of worrying about her own problems, went to help her cousin Elizabeth. Then, after three months, she came back home again.

Later, about nine months after she had been visited by the angel, she and Joseph had to take another trip. Augustus Caesar, the emperor of the Roman empire, decreed that there would be a census over the whole world. Everyone was to go to the city of his ancestors to register for the census.

The village of Bethlehem was the home of Joseph's and Mary's ancestors, for they were from the tribe of Judah. So Mary and Joseph traveled to Bethlehem to register. When they arrived there, they found that there was no room in the inn. They ended up spending the night in a cave where the animals were kept.

That night Mary gave birth to her Baby, a Boy, Whom they named Jesus, the name that He had been given by the Archangel Gabriel.

At that moment, angels appeared to a group of shepherds who were watching their sheep in the fields. The angels told them about Jesus' birth, and they left their sheep and went to the cave to pay homage to this newborn King.

Jewish Parents

JOSEPH and Mary were good Jewish parents. They observed the law that God had given to Moses and Israel. They kept the feasts of Israel with great reverence.

Thus, when Jesus was eight days old, they had Him circumcised. This was an ancient custom in Israel. It was a sign of God's promise to Abraham. Yahweh would be Abraham's God, and Abraham and his descendants would be His people. By having Jesus circumcised, Joseph and Mary were making Jesus part of that covenant.

Then, forty days after Jesus was born, Joseph and Mary and the Baby went to the temple in Jerusalem. The Jewish law required that mothers who had just given birth be purified, and this ceremony took place forty days after the birth of her Child.

Also, since Jesus was a firstborn, His family had to offer a sacrifice to redeem Him. God had saved all of the firstborn of the people of Israel from the angel of death when He brought His people out of Egypt. From then on, they belonged to God.

People would therefore offer a small sacrifice to buy these children back. Since Joseph and Mary were poor, they offered the sacrifice of the poor, two small birds.

Signs of the Future

THAT day in the temple, Mary and Joseph received a sign that foretold the future of their Son. Simeon and Anna announced that He would be the Savior of Israel. Simeon also told Mary that a sword would pierce her heart.

Sometime after this, astrologers arrived from the East to pay tribute to the newborn King of the Jews. They had learned of Jesus' birth from the stars.

They first went to the palace of King Herod, but after he consulted with his counselors, they went to Bethlehem, where the Holy Family was staying.

These Magi brought gifts for the newborn King. They brought Him gold, frankincense, and myrrh. Gold was the gift that one would be expected to give to a king, and frankincense is a type of incense, something that gives honor to God. Finally, myrrh is used to prepare a dead body for its burial. This gift was a sign that Jesus would die to free us from our sins.

King Herod was very evil, and he wanted to kill the newborn Baby. He sent soldiers to kill all of the small children who were living in that area. But Joseph was once again visited by an angel in a dream. The angel warned him to take the Holy Family to Egypt to save them from the plot of the evil king.

A Normal Family

A COUPLE of years later, the Holy Family heard that King Herod had died. They could now move back home. But they found out that King Herod's son was ruling in Judea, and he was even worse than his father. So the Holy Family set out for Galilee in the north. They traveled to the town of Nazareth, where Jesus grew up.

This was a very poor town, so poor that most people did not even have houses in which they could live. They lived in caves in the hillsides. It was so poor that one of Jesus' disciples would later say, "What good can come from Nazareth?"

The family of Jesus was even poorer than most. Joseph was a carpenter. In those days, everyone wanted to own some land and be a farmer. If one was a carpenter, it meant that his family did not even have any land on which they could grow their own crops.

But Joseph worked hard and earned a living for his family. He also taught Jesus how to be a carpenter. Later on, people would call Jesus both "the Son of the carpenter" and "the Carpenter," for He was both.

From all that we know, the Holy Family lived a quiet life in Nazareth.

Lost in the Temple

THERE was really only one event during these years that disturbed their quiet lives. This happened when Jesus was twelve years old.

It was a Jewish custom to go up to Jerusalem three times a year for feasts if one lived close enough to the temple and could afford the trip. We hear that the Holy Family were good Jews who observed the Jewish law, and we also know that they made the pilgrimage to Jerusalem at least once a year, for the Feast of the Passover.

One of those times, Joseph and Mary lost track of Him as they set out to return home. Joseph thought Jesus was traveling with His mother (for men and women often traveled in separate groups), and Mary thought that He was traveling with Joseph.

After a while, they realized that Jesus was not with either of them, so they returned to Jerusalem. They searched for Him for three days. They eventually found Him in the temple, listening to and speaking with the doctors of the law as they discussed how to live the law of Moses in their everyday lives. The people who were standing nearby were amazed at His wisdom, for He understood the deepest meaning of the law: love.

The Death of Joseph

MARY and Joseph were very disturbed that Jesus had been lost for three days. Mary asked Jesus how He could do this to her and Joseph. But Jesus answered, "Did you not know that I had to be about My Father's business?" He was reminding them that God was His Father, and the day would come when He would leave them to do God's work.

So Jesus returned to Nazareth with Joseph and Mary, and He grew in wisdom and grace before God and before others.

We do not know exactly when it happened, but it seems as if Joseph died sometime afterward, probably before Jesus began His public ministry. We believe this because when people spoke about Jesus they called Him the Son of Mary. In those days, one was always called the son of one's father until the father died, and only then the son of one's mother. (Remember, while we know that Joseph was only Jesus' foster father and that God was Jesus' real Father, the people who lived in His village did not know this. They believed that Joseph was His real father.)

We do know one thing about Joseph's death. If he died with Jesus and Mary at his side, then he died at peace. This is why we pray to St. Joseph for a peaceful death.

Jesus' Public Ministry

AFTER the death of Joseph, Jesus continued to care for His mother. He earned a living, using the skills as a carpenter that His foster father Joseph had taught Him.

Then, when He was about thirty years old, He set out to begin His public ministry. In those days, a man would not be considered to be a teacher of the law, a rabbi, until he was thirty. When Jesus had reached that age, people would be willing to listen to Him and to take Him seriously. It was time for Him to proclaim the kingdom of God.

Jesus must have entrusted His mother to His relatives living in Nazareth. This was not unusual, for in those days cousins often took care of relatives who did not have anyone else to care for them.

It must have been difficult for Jesus to leave His mother this way. He would probably have preferred to take care of her Himself, but God had called Him to preach God's word of consolation and conversion. He had to be obedient to His Father's will. He even taught that one has to be willing to leave everyone and everything in order to follow God's call.

Every once in a while Mary seems to have visited Jesus, but most of the time she probably stayed at home and hoped and prayed for her beloved Son.

The Wedding Feast at Cana

ONE of the times that Mary was with Jesus was when they were invited to attend a wedding feast in Cana of Galilee. This was a town not all that far away from Nazareth.

During the feast Mary noticed that the newly married couple had run out of wine. This would have been a terrible embarrassment. The entire village would have been invited to the wedding, and they would have gossiped about this for a long, long time.

Mary went over to Jesus and told Him to do something. He responded, "What is it to you and Me, woman? My hour has not yet come." This sounds like Jesus was talking back to His mother, but it was not like that. In the language that Jesus spoke, it simply meant that it was none of their business.

Yet, Mary told the servants to do whatever Jesus told them to do. She knew that her Son was too generous not to help the couple.

Jesus had the servants fill six large stone jars with water, and He changed the water into wine. When the head waiter tasted the new wine, he was very surprised for it was even better than the first wine that they had served.

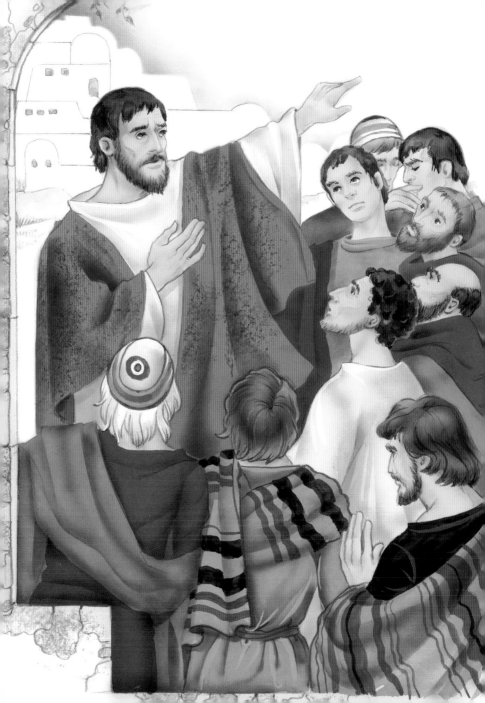

Jesus Preaches in the Synagogue in Nazareth

JESUS performed many miracles during His public ministry.

Once, when He was crossing the Sea of Galilee with His disciples, a great storm blew up and their boat was at the point of sinking. In the meantime, Jesus had fallen asleep in the boat. The disciples woke Jesus up and begged Him to do something. He ordered the wind to be calm, and the storm immediately stopped.

As soon as they landed on the shore, they were met by a man who had an evil spirit. Its name was Legion, meaning that there were many evil spirits in the man. Jesus ordered them to come out of the man, and he was healed.

Jesus then met Jairus, whose daughter was dying. Jairus asked Jesus to heal his daughter. On his way to Jairus's house Jesus healed a woman who had been sick for twelve years. Then, when he arrived at Jairus's house, Jesus raised his daughter from the dead.

After all this, when Jesus preached in the synagogue in His hometown of Nazareth, His family and friends rejected Him. Sometimes we cannot see and appreciate the good in people when we know them too well, and that is what seems to have happened to Jesus.

Behold Your Mother

THE next time that we hear about Mary is when she was standing under the Cross. We see how much Jesus loved His mother, for even while He was dying, He was thinking of her and who would take care of her when He was gone.

The beloved disciple was standing under the Cross alongside of Mary. He loved Jesus so much that he refused to run away when the other disciples had fled out of fear.

Jesus looked down at the beloved disciple and His mother and said, "Woman, behold your son." He then said to the beloved disciple, "Son, behold your mother." From then on, the beloved disciple cared for Mary as he would have cared for his own mother.

There was also another meaning to these words. Jesus loved the Church so much that He died for us on the Cross. It was such a great love that people said it was as if He were marrying the Church.

In Israel, when a man died without having children, his brother would marry the widow to have children in his name. The beloved disciple was now Jesus' brother. He was to marry the Church (love and care for it) so that it could have many children who would be called by His name: Christians.

Mary at Pentecost

MARY must have suffered terribly when Jesus died on the Cross. She had only one consolation when she buried Him. She could remember that He had been lost in Jerusalem for three days when He was about His Father's business. Now, He was lost again.

Then, on the third day, she received the news that Jesus had been raised from the dead. Her joy must have been tremendous. Her beloved Son was alive.

Forty days later, Jesus ascended into heaven. Even though Jesus was gone again, she could trust. She had seen God do great things, and she knew that Jesus was not going away forever.

Mary joined the Apostles to pray in the upper room, the place where Jesus had celebrated the Last Supper with His Apostles. They were praying there ten days later on the Feast of Pentecost, when the Holy Spirit descended upon them in the form of tongues of fire.

This was the birth of the Church. From then on, the Apostles had the courage to proclaim Jesus' message wherever they went. In so doing, they could always reflect upon the example of Mary, whose love and generosity made it possible for Jesus to be born into this world.

The Assumption

AFTER Pentecost, the Apostles and disciples preached the Good News in countries all over the face of the earth. They announced that Jesus had died for our sins and that God had raised Him from the dead.

It was around this time that the beloved disciple took Mary with him when he traveled to the city of Ephesus in southern Turkey. One can still see the house in which they lived.

Some people say that they stayed there for the rest of their lives, and others say that they moved back to Jerusalem for a while. We are just not all that sure. All we know is that the beloved disciple obeyed Jesus' command, and he took care of Mary with great love.

Then, when Mary's life on earth had come to an end, God granted her a special favor. He took her up into heaven, body and soul. We call this the Assumption.

Through this miracle, God was showing us the love He had for Mary, and He was also showing us what His love would do to each one of us one day. At the end of the world, we will all rise from the dead and, if we have lived in God's love, we will be taken home to heaven to live with God forever, body and soul.

Devotion to Joseph and Mary

JESUS grew up in a family that taught Him the true meaning of love.

Mary became His mother because she was so loving that she offered herself to God as His servant.

Joseph was so loving that he broke the law in order to care for Mary and Jesus.

The Holy Family did not have it easy, but they always trusted in God's plan.

We pray for their intercession for our families. May our homes be like the Holy Family's home in Nazareth.